Lafayette Carthon Musicians' HandBook 2nd Edition

Lafayette Carthon Musicians' HandBook 2nd Edition

FOR MUSIC LOVERS EVERYWHERE

Lafayette Carthon

Lafayette Carthon
Musicians' Handbook

2nd Edition

for music lovers everywhere

The Official Handbook for:

Carthon Conservatory
540 East 105th Street Suite 210 Cleveland, Oh 44108
www.carthonconservatory.com

Lafayette Carthon Musicians' Handbook Copyright © 2006, © 2015

Cover design by Delon Stradford (Digital Hard Copy, LLC)
Edit/proofread by Kris Ashley (Belvedere Editorial & Research)

All rights reserved. This publication is protected by Copyright and permission should be obtained from the publisher prior to any reproduction, storage in a retrieval system, or transmission in any form or by any means, electric, mechanical, photocopying, recording or otherwise. For information regarding permission, visit us at www.carthon.org or write to us at the address above.
Unauthorized reproduction of this publication is prohibited by Federal Law.

Scripture marked KJV is taken from the Holy Bible, King James Version. Public Domain.

Scripture marked MSG is taken from *The Message*. Copyright© by Eugene H. Peterson, 1993, 1994, 1995, 1996, 2000, 2001, 2002. Used by permission of NavPress Publishing Group.

Scripture marked NIV is taken from the Holy Bible, New International Version®, NIV® Copyright © 1973, 1978, 1984, 2010 by Biblica, Inc.™ Used by permission. All rights reserved worldwide.

Scripture marked NLT is taken from the Holy Bible, New Living Translation, copyright 1996, 2004. Used by permission of Tyndale House Publishers, Inc., Wheaton, Illinois 60189. All rights reserved.

ISBN-13: 9781480202078
ISBN-10: 148020207X
Library of Congress Control Number: 2015915780
CreateSpace Independent Publishing Platform
North Charleston, South carolina

Other books by Lafayette Carthon

Eat, Breathe, Drink: Three keys to unstoppable faith

(Coming soon)

Chord Progressions for Modern Worship

(Coming soon)

Anything You Can Do I Can Do Better: The superiority of Jesus Christ

(Coming Soon)

**Visit carthon.org to order copies of this book for your church, school, group or private students. Discounts available for bulk orders.
Help us change a generation of musicians!**

This book is dedicated to my parents,
who sacrificed to pay for my private music lessons.

About the Author

An Oberlin Conservatory Graduate and Moody Bible College Alumnus, Lafayette Carthon is an award winning musician whose music production and keyboarding skills can be heard on many gold and platinum-selling music projects with Grammy Award Winning Artists, including Celine Dion, The Winans, Mary J. Blige, Michael Jackson, Trisha Yearwood, R-Kelly, The Isley Brothers and many others (Allmusic.com; PBS Television; The Cleveland Plain Dealer). He is Founder of Carthon Conservatory and Senior Pastor of Faith Church of Glenville, in Cleveland, Ohio (faithchurchofglenville.org). He is the author of this handbook, which is the culminating work of more than 25 years of research and experience in the music industry and in church ministry.

As a young child, Lafayette Carthon studied under the tutelage of Jeanette Steele—a distinguished pianist in the Church of God in Christ tradition—and later under Dr. William B. Woods—a renowned choral conductor. Under their watchful eye he honed his skills as a composer/arranger and a classical and jazz pianist. He studied at the Cleveland Institute of Music and later graduated from the prestigious Oberlin Conservatory of Music.

Today, Lafayette Carthon is living-out-loud his passion for youth music education through the P.s.a.l.m.i.s.t. Program, which stands for:

Perfecting Singers Artists Linguists & Musicians Impacting Society Today

The P.s.a.l.m.i.s.t. Program is the flagship program and core curriculum of Mr. Carthon's music school (Carthon Conservatory). The P.s.a.l.m.i.s.t. Program helps develop young musicians in a holistic way (musically and spiritually). Carthon Conservatory is a community music and technology center headquartered in Cleveland, Ohio, which has been dubbed the "YMCA of music."

With a 200-city vision, Carthon Conservatory continues to partner with teachers and K-12 schools to incorporate the P.s.a.l.m.i.s.t. Program into their curriculums. To date, The P.s.a.l.m.i.s.t. Program has been adopted in whole or in part by many schools and institutions of higher learning, and can be integrated into any music program—public or private. (For more details visit www.psalmistprogram.org).

Contents

Preface · xv

Carthon Conservatory Music Creed · · · · · · · · · · · · · xvii

Introduction · xix

Music Purpose · xxi

1. A Passion for Music · xxi

2. Gift-Sitting · xxii

3. Write this Down · xxiii

4. The Recorder · xxv

5. Belief in Action · xxvi

6. The Three P's (Prayer, Practice, Performance) · · xxviii

Part 1 1

    Music Worship 3

    1. The Vertical 3

    2. Hearing Beyond Sound 5

    3. My Number One Fan 6

    4. PWM & CCM 9

    5. Balance Your Music 12

    6. Publishing History 14

    7. God Affirms and Qualifies 15

    8. Private Performance 16

    9. Two Way Street 16

    10. Investing in Music 20

    11. Multiple Revenue Streams 22

    12. Respecting the Home Front 23

13. Don't Forget Your Hymns · 27

14. Royal Etiquette · 30

Part 2 · 33

Music Entertainment · 35

1. The Horizontal · 35

2. Love Songs · 37

3. An Opportunity · 39

4. Get Wisdom! · 41

5. Staying Power · 42

6. Content Management · 44

7. Promotion · 45

8. Compliments and Criticism · · · · · · · · · · · · · · · · · · · 46

9. Recap: Perfecting Music Entertainment · · · · · · · · · 47

Part 3 ··· 51

    Music Teaching ···························· 53

    1. Making Musicians ······················· 53

    2. Honor Your Teachers ···················· 55

    3. A Gift to Teach ························· 56

    4. The Money Myth ······················· 59

    5. The Degree Myth ······················· 61

    6. Actions Teach Louder Than Words ·············· 61

    7. Message Carrier ························ 63

    8. Reading Music and Playing by Ear ··············· 64

    9. Music in Other People's Heads ················· 66

    10. Conclusion ··························· 69

    For bookings, visit carthon.org

Preface

In the beginning God created the heavens and the earth (Genesis 1:1). I believe this wholeheartedly, which is to say that God made everything, including music. From the air we breathe to the songs we sing, everything that has been made was made by God, and all things belong to Him (John 1:1-3).

Because God made music, no human being can truly be at his or her best performing or teaching music without consulting with God. As the Creator of music, God knows best how music should work, and how it should be taught, practiced, marketed and performed. I, and all musicians, would do well to be in awe of God, and to approach doing music with an attitude of prayer, humility and thanksgiving. There are no human geniuses in music, only musicians who allow the genius of God to flow through them.

Consequently, it is with humility that I write this book and share some of the ubiquitous truths about music from a biblical perspective; truths that I have discovered to be timeless. I believe that these truths are relevant to musicians and artists of all types, everywhere.

To musicians my age, I write this book and speak to you with the respect I would my own brothers and sisters. To musicians 20 years or older than me, I speak to you with the respect I would an uncle, mother or even a father (1 Timothy 5:1-2). You've been around much longer than me, and therefore, deserve such respect. And to musicians and youth 20 years younger than me, I speak to you with the care and concern I would my own nieces and nephews, even my own children (Ephesians 6:4).

Whatever your age, I pray that as you read you will be refreshed and encouraged to more faithfully pursue your God-given purpose in life and in music, and in that order. I believe there is so much more, even beyond music, which God has planned for all of us who seek Him. So don't limit yourself.

I conclude with the words to a song I penned many years ago, which says:

Maximize this moment. It may not come again. Trust in God, believe that you can; you can do all things, through Christ Jesus. Maximize this moment, you can.

-Lafayette Carthon

Carthon Conservatory Music Creed

There are only three things I can do with music. I can worship with it, entertain with it, or teach it. Music worship means performing my best for God. Music entertainment means performing my best for people, and music teaching means teaching others how to do both of the above, correctly and with integrity. There is a right way to do music and a wrong way. I choose to do music the right way.

-Lafayette Carthon 2006 ©

Introduction

(Advanced musicians and artists can skip this section, if desired)

Music Purpose

1. A Passion for Music

Do you have a passion for music? Do you love to play an instrument, sing or write songs and you want to do more to further your music? Well, that is no accident, my friend. Your passion for music was given to you by the Maker of Music, God, and He doesn't make mistakes.

The truth is, you don't have to be a professional musician, singer or songwriter to pursue your passion for music. Why? Because music was made for everyone. That means you! What's more is that there are many ways you can fulfill your music passion and purpose. So don't say things like "I can't do it" or "I'm not good enough" or "I'm too old." You *can* do it! And you're not too old or too young. With proper guidance and effort you can be on your way to furthering your music.

Even if you're already an accomplished musician or successful recording artist there is still more you can achieve, and this book contains valuable information that can help you.

Never forget, you have a musical contribution to make to this world. Yes, you! And you don't have to make a choice between doing music or spending time with family or friends or pursuing a career or any other thing. You can do all of the above and more. Yes, you can multi-task! So do your music! Don't leave this earth having never fulfilled your musical purpose. Take time now to focus on it. It may be one of your true callings.

2. Gift-Sitting

People often say, "…if you don't use your talent you will lose it." That, my friend, is a lie. The Maker of Music gave you your gift. He gave you your talent. His gifts are irrevocable, meaning He doesn't take them back (Romans 11:29). So what really happens when you don't use your music gift? It gets rusty! That's what happens!

Think of it like this: Suppose someone gives you a new car that you never drive. Instead, you let the car sit in your garage for 20 years. Is the car still yours? Yes, but chances are it won't run very well, if at all, because it's been sitting for so long. In order to get the car on the road again, it will require some work.

Well… if your talent is like that car, unused for many years, I have good news for you. It's not too late to get your talent back on the road again! No matter how rusty your talent may be or whether you're just starting out in music, your musical talent hasn't been taken from you. You simply need to begin using it. This will require work, but you can do it. You can do all things through Christ (Philippians 4:13). So, no more gift-sitting. Get up! Start moving forward. Work with what you have.

3. Write this Down

Describe your music passion in detail. Don't just say it but write it down. Make it plain. In your own words explain what it is you feel driven to do. How would you best describe the music you've been hearing in your mind? What types of musical sounds ignite your passion the most? Make a note of it, because those are clues to your music purpose.

What about lyrics and poetry writing? Do you find yourself putting together words that express your feelings and convictions? Do you think some of those words could be put to music? Perhaps.

Whatever the case is, take time to express your thoughts in writing. Think about where and how you want to improve yourself musically. You don't have to start big; you can begin with something as simple as learning how to more effectively manage your practice time. Perhaps you want to get a better grasp on music theory or develop your understanding of chords and harmony. Maybe you want to learn the keyboard, guitar or some other instrument or maybe you feel drawn to the behind-the-scene area of music, such as music-production, engineering, marketing or management.

In any case, put these thoughts and ideas down on paper or in your tablet or phone. These written notes can help provide a roadmap for you; one that will help you focus on the goal of improving yourself musically. Having a roadmap and plan will help you be more intentional about your music, to do music on purpose and not just sit back and *see* what happens.

Keep a journal and update it as necessary. Include benchmarks (smaller goals along the way) and milestones (larger goals), which is a good way to evaluate your progress. Pray and make plans, and be sure to do the daily things necessary to live out your plan. Use the space below to begin formulating your thoughts.

_____
_____
_____
_____
_____
_____
_____
_____
_____
_____
_____
_____
_____
_____
_____
_____
_____

4. The Recorder

Now that you've written down some thoughts concerning your music, it's time to record. No, I don't mean going into a professional recording studio (unless you have it like that!). Instead, use an electronic voice-recorder to record any melodies or musical ideas you may be working on. (There are several mobile apps that you can use to record your voice.) The point is to preserve and protect your ideas.

Let me caution you. Many great songs and musical ideas have been lost because some people, after hearing music in their heads, failed to record it or put it down on paper. Thinking they would remember later, to their disappointment, they did not. Other people have had their ideas and concepts stolen because they shared their ideas before they were copyrighted. But even if your ideas are copyrighted, it's not always good to share them with others prematurely.

So make provisions to record and protect your music, but without going to extremes. You don't want to become paranoid and suspicious of everyone, and start believing that everyone is out to steal your music. That would be immature, and might make you a pain to be around. But by the same token, you want to take reasonable precautions by copyrighting music you plan to do in public.

If you plan on performing your music publicly, then you can cut down on expenses by copyrighting all of your songs as a single collection and pay only one fee. Copyright laws and policies are subject to change so be sure to contact the Library of Congress to get the latest news on copyright guidelines. As of the printing of this book, copyrighting songs as a collection costs between $35-$60 total, which beats paying $60 per song! You can copyright your music online by going to https://eco.copyright.gov and registering your original works (i.e. songs, poetry, etc.). If you prefer the mail, the address is: U.S. Copyright Office 101 Independence Avenue SE Washington, DC 20559-6000. The phone number is (202) 707-3000. Again, this information is subject to change, so be sure to double check before you send.

It's not necessary to spend tons of money on music production just to copyright your completed songs, but make sure all recordings you submit are of good quality. If you feel the need, you can find a local professional musician and/or singer to assist you in completing a basic recording of your music. Lastly, be sure to consult with at least two or three professional songwriters who have recently copyrighted music the correct way, not the "poor man's" copyright way. The "poor man's" copyright is when a person mails an original recording of a song to his or herself and doesn't open the envelope; thus "proving" the date it was written. Unfortunately, this "poor man's" way of copyrighting music is not legal and won't hold up in a court of law.

5. Belief in Action

Now that you've expressed your passion on paper and have recorded your musical ideas (so not to forget them), it's time to pull out your calendar. Fulfilling your music passion and purpose will require a little planning. You'll never reach your potential without setting some dates.

Reaching your music goals is going to require two things:

- Your persistent *belief* that you have a musical purpose

- Your persistent *action* to fulfill that purpose

The fact that you're reading this book suggests you believe there's a purpose for your music, and that you're willing to take action to pursue that purpose. That means you're not just a talker, but a doer. And that's a good thing, because talk is not cheap. I repeat. Talk is *not* cheap. On the contrary, talk is very expensive because if all you do is talk about fulfilling your musical purpose, but never take action, you will miss out on what you were purposed to do musically. And that, my friend, would be a very expensive mistake.

So, whether you're a full-time student, full-time employee, entrepreneur or retiree you can make smart moves to grow and advance yourself in music. There's no need to become stressed or overworked in the process. Making music should be fun and enjoyable, not stressful and overbearing. That doesn't mean you won't face challenges. But there should be a measure of peace and personal fulfillment that comes with making music, in spite of challenges. Only do not sit there and do nothing. Make a conscious effort to further your music daily.

6. The Three P's (Prayer, Practice, Performance)

Pray

If you believe gifts and talents come from God, then you should have no problem with the Three P's. That's prayer, practice, and performance. For sure, if you neglect to pray and ask for direction from the Maker of Music—God, you will most certainly begin on a bad note. (Pun intended)

Failing to pray concerning your music, means that you're choosing to do things your own way. That's fine, if you'd like. But know this; if you try to go it alone you will invariably make some very bad decisions musically, personally and otherwise. Without help, your efforts will slowly begin to degrade in one way or another. Sure, it may appear that some musicians and artists are getting along fine without prayer, but that's only part of the picture. Sooner or later they will encounter some challenges that will require help that goes beyond human resources. When that happens, things will come crashing down for them. The same will happen to you if you don't make prayer a priority.

Having worked in the music business for many years, and had the pleasure of doing music keyboard work on projects with Michael Jackson, Celine Dion, The Winans, Mary J. Blige, R-Kelly and many others, I can honestly say that no one will *truly* do well for long in the music industry without personal help from God.

Trust me. The music industry is chock-full of performers who don't pray or pay God any attention, and as a result many of them have made some awful business decisions, ruined good relationships and even compromised their artistic integrity for little or nothing. Some have suffered great financial loss and others have sunk to the point of moral bankruptcy, giving the best of themselves to people who couldn't care less. Further still, some have paid the ultimate price for their mistakes, having met with some tragic end.

Here's the good news. That doesn't have to happen to you! You can protect yourself by praying to God, the Maker of Music. Tell Him what's on your mind and ask for His direction. Listen closely to Him through His Word, the Bible. If you do so, you will develop the faith and the spiritual lifeskills necessary to handle the day-to-day madness in and around the music industry. (For more on prayer, read Part 2 in *Eat, Breathe, Drink: Three keys to unstoppable faith*)

Practice

Secondly, if you believe in prayer then you know that God is no slacker, but requires us to do our very best. To do our best means we must practice.

Practice is essential to developing your music skills. There's no getting around it. It doesn't matter how well you sing, play or write songs you must make time to practice if you're going to grow and get better. You must study your craft. Even if you're extremely gifted naturally, God requires that you grow and study to better yourself (2 Peter 3:18; 2 Timothy 2:15; Psalm 33:3). That means you can be better than everyone around you and still get a failing grade from God! Why? He grades you based on how well you've maximized the talent He's given you, not on how much better you are compared to other people.

Maximizing your talent in a healthy, holistic way is the main point of practicing. Designate a space in your home for practicing and writing music, a space with some privacy so you don't disturb family members or neighbors. Responsibly invest in music lessons and in the instruments and/or equipment you need. Be economically prudent in your purchases. If you are a teen student, you should work a summer job, if possible, to help cover costs associated with your music. This promotes responsibility.

Whatever your age, practice at home and be on time for rehearsals outside of your home. Find a teacher/mentor that is a good fit—someone highly skilled, with a good reputation who loves to teach. Use local and online resources to meet your music needs. You can find hundreds of beginner-keyboard tutorials on the Lafayette Carthon YouTube to get you started. Developing good practice habits take time, so don't cut corners, and don't rely on music tutorials alone. Great musicianship requires great mentorship, so be sure to connect with a real-life teacher or artist(s) who can help you shape your artistry. Take advantage of any and all proven resources available to further your musical development.

Perform

Thirdly, if you believe that prayer and practice are a necessity, then you can't stop there, but you absolutely must perform, even if only at home for yourself or for family and friends. Don't just talk about doing music. *Do* music. Use your gift(s) and talent(s) in a tangible, positive way. Join an existing band, choir or other performing arts group or start your own if that's the route you want to go. Take part in school performances and community music concerts. You can perform for seniors and youths or do talent shows and recitals. If you're a songwriter, that is all the more reason to perform for live audiences, because performing your own music gives you a platform to have your music heard.

Whether you're a youth or adult, you need to perform and keep performing. It's never too late. Ever heard of Suzan Boyle? She became an international music star overnight, after auditioning on the talent show *Britain's Got Talent*. But guess how old she was? 48! Yes, 48 years old! This goes to show you that anything is possible with a little bit of faith and a whole lot of practice! So, don't let age, lack of resources, or anything else prevent you from actively performing your music. Pray, practice, and get out there and perform!

Notes

Part 1

Music Worship

1. The Vertical

So here it is in a nutshell. After nearly 30 years in the music industry, I learned that "there are only three things I can do with music. I can worship with it, entertain with it, or teach it. Music worship means performing my best for God. Music entertainment means performing my best for people, and music teaching means teaching others how to do both of the above, correctly and with integrity. There is a right way to do music and a wrong way. I choose to do music the right way" (Carthon, 2006).

I copyrighted the saying above in 2006, which is the year Carthon Conservatory (*formerly Carthon Academy*) was born. The three things just mentioned (worship, entertainment, and teaching) are essential to developing good musicianship. The order in which they appear is also essential, which is why we begin with worship.

Worshipping with music is listed first because it is, and should always be, the first thing musicians learn to do in music. Johann Sebastian Bach—arguably the greatest Western Music composer of all times—was a worshipper. He was also a church organist, and between him and Art Tatum they are my favorite keyboardists. Musical worship is a vertical act directed towards God, who is the Maker of Music. Honoring God first in your music—that is putting Him first in your life—makes the most sense because God is not only the Maker of Music but also the Maker of everything, even you! It is God who allows you to breathe, and He holds your life in His hands. So honor Him first. Worship Him in spirit and in truth. Let your music be one of many ways you give thanks to God, not the only way.

But one word of warning. Music worship can be easily misunderstood, and as a result many people have had botched attempts at doing worship music because they approached it the wrong way. The reason for this is that many musicians and artists have not been properly taught how God, according to the Bible, intends for worship music to be performed. Also, many musicians have applied pop-culture standards to musical worship, which is totally the wrong way to approach it.

Listen. Music worship is not about how well you play, sing or write songs. It's not about fame, popularity or how much money you make. It's not about how much you spend on musical instruments, equipment, recording or promotion of your music. And it's not even about how religious or spiritual you think your music is. Rather, music worship is about one thing and one thing only. Relationship.

Yes, *relationship*. And that relationship has to do with you (the performer) and your audience of one (God). This makes music worship a vertical act, not a horizontal act. It makes it a God-centered act, not a people-centered act. That means if your music worship is focused on pleasing people and not pleasing God, your music worship is wrong—dead wrong, no matter how wonderful it may sound.

There is much more that we will cover on the subject of doing music worship. But for now, remember this: Before you engage in worship music _for_ God, be sure you have a relationship _with_ God. No relationship, no worship. It's that simple.

2. Hearing Beyond Sound

The reason many musicians and artist mess up music worship is they don't understand God or how He hears music, which is easy to do if you don't have a real relationship with Him.

First, you should know that God's listening goes deeper and far beyond mere audio sound. He in fact is able to go behind the music and listen to the motives of a performer's heart. That means when you do music worship, God focuses on the intent in your mind, not the chords you play or the riffs you sing. He tunes in to your personal character and listens closely to your heart's true ambitions. The specific notes you play or sing are mere music packaging to God, like the shrink-wrapping on a CD. We all know that CD-wrapping is not the actual music, not the thing people ultimately want. Neither are the notes you play the thing that God ultimately wants. The real music is what's *on* the CD, not what's on the cover. Likewise, real music worship begins with what's in your *heart*, not what's in the *notes* you perform.

God can never be impressed by the notes you, me or anyone plays or sings. Remember, He is the Maker of Music—the actual Architect of Music! There is no note that any performer can ever play or sing that will astonish or amaze Him. He made all notes! But what *does* impress Him when you play or sing is the <u>high-pitched sound</u> that a life lived with integrity produces. He loves to hear that! What also impresses Him is the <u>mid-range sound</u> that forgiveness and loving one's enemies produces. God is big on forgiveness and love, so much so that He sacrificed His own Son on account of it (John 3:16). And lastly, what impresses God in your music is the <u>deep, rich sound</u> of faith in Christ—faith to believe that anything is possible if you only trust Him and not give up hope.

If you put those high sounds (integrity), midrange sounds (forgiveness), and low sounds (faith) together, you are sure to perform worship music the right way, and create a sweet sound that is pleasing to God's ears; a sound that only He can fully appreciate.

3. My Number One Fan

In one sense, performing worship music seems like a reasonable thing to do. But in another sense, it seems totally ridiculous. Why?

Performing worship music means performing for the supreme music perfectionist of all time—God. How ridiculous is that! It means performing for the One who actually invented music. Think about that for a moment... God is the One who designed melody, harmony, counterpoint, chord progressions, tonality and atonality. He is the Maker of Music!

Consider this. Not only can God hear the notes you play and sing right now, but God can actually recall every note you have ever played or sung! I'm not making this up. In fact, the Bible is clear that God keeps up with the smallest details of your life, even the exact number of hairs on your head (Luke 12:1). If He keeps up with the hairs on your head, then you know He keeps up with the notes and melodies you offer to Him through praise and worship. (This would be an excellent time to pause, put down this book and give God praise for His attention to the smallest details of your life!)

Please understand this. No one, I mean no one, should make you more nervous to perform for than God, because no person living or dead knows more about music than Him, and no one keeps up with the musical details of your life like Him. Don't believe me? Name a note. Go ahead. Name any note you want, A^b, C, D, $E^\#$, it doesn't matter. God can tell you exactly how many times you have ever performed that note, and He can tell you where you were at the time. He can also tell you whether or not the note you played or sung was in tune! Are you getting this, really getting it? God's memory power is so high and inestimable that He, if He wanted to, could tell you what the temperature was outside at the time you performed the note. He knows the exact amount of skill and energy it took for you to produce that single note, and what it will take for you to do it again and again. In fact, God could tell you the amount of skill and energy it has taken for every musician in every nation of every century to produce a musical sound on any instrument at anytime and in any place. But I'm still not sure if you're getting this.

Listen. God can tell you, note for note and pitch for pitch, the melodic sequences of every song ever uttered by human beings (and birds too) from the beginning of the world until now, and without breaking a sweat transpose every song into all twelve keys, including the micro-semitones in between keys. And just for fun, He can create a complex fugue using all 12 notes arranged in 12 part counterpoint, which would make the music of Bach and Mozart sound like "Chopsticks"!

You see? There is no one in the universe you should be more intimidated to perform for than God. No one. This is why you should approach the performance of worship music with reverence and awe. Never be smug or arrogant and approach music worship in a flippant manner. To do so is not only naïve but dangerously disrespectful.

God is the Author of life, the Maker of not only music, but of all things. Yet, unlike some of the mean-spirited talent-show judges today, God is the kindest audience member for whom you could ever perform. He knows everything there is to know about you—the good, the bad and the ugly—but in spite of that, He still loves you! He is your number one fan—<u>a fan of the new Christ-centered you</u>, not the old unbelieving you! No one supports your musical purpose like God. And why wouldn't He support it, after all, He gave you that purpose! So relax. You won't hear God verbally bashing you in public about your musical short-comings, which is not to suggest that He is passive or weak. Don't misunderstand. God is not a fan of spiritual mediocrity or musical mediocrity, but prefers that we are hot or cold, not lukewarm (Revelation 3:15-16). He demands excellence. He demands our very best. However, He also knows your beginning from the end, and He sees that your best days are still ahead. He knows that you and I are a work in progress!

So don't give up. Keep pursuing your musical purpose in God and perfecting your music skills. And don't be lazy, cut corners or make excuses for not growing or getting better in music. Trust me. God will know if you're being lazy, so don't waste time with excuses. Sharpen your gifts, talents and abilities. All of them. You're not in competition with the person next to you. You're in competition with excellence! And yes God requires excellence. So be diligent, hardworking, humble, and most of all faithful.

4. PWM & CCM

The most profound principle behind PWM (Praise & Worship Music) and CCM (Contemporary Christian Music) can be found in the prayer of Jesus, "Father make them one, even as we are one" (John 17:21). The point is that PWM (the term used more for urban sacred music) and CCM (the term used more for suburban sacred music) is merely one more medium through which God is making us "one." And by "us" I mean those people, regardless of church affiliation or denomination, who have faith in God and His Son, Jesus Christ.

Know this. God is tearing down racial barriers and denominational walls through music, among other things. He is causing songwriters to simplify chord progressions on the PWM side (vi, IV, I, V) and adding a little gospel flair on the CCM side (IV^{Maj7}, $III^{7(\#9)}$, vi, II^7). Not only that, He is saturating urban and suburban worship music with scripture. Songwriters are creating modern canticles (i.e. songs incorporating words directly from the Bible) in increasing quantities. These things are happening so that we may become one, and speak with one voice-one sound.

That doesn't mean all worship music should sound the same or be limited to 3 or 4 chords. The world is too big and God's plan is too vast to limit worship music to any one genre, instrument, person, place or thing.

The point is that God uses an innumerable amount of musical styles, methods, mediums and techniques to engage us in worship and to advance His kingdom plan for us and for all people. PWM and CCM are merely two of many ways God is using to further His agenda to break down barriers and promote unity among all Believers. Jesus prayed, "Make them one" (John 17:21), and we know God's Word cannot be voided or cancelled (Isaiah 55:11).

Therefore, God is going to make us one (in love) whether some like it or not. He is stripping many of our church services down to the bare essentials, ridding our public worship experiences of unnecessary ritualistic practices that have little to do with perfecting our faith in Him. But don't misunderstand. There is nothing wrong with certain ceremonial practices or "tradition" in the church. Tradition merely means customs or beliefs that are transmitted from generation to generation. And that is something we should do. However, there is such a thing as good tradition and bad tradition. And we should strive to incorporate good tradition, the kind founded on the principles of God's Word.

So, in the spirit of oneness, I am releasing a new music book entitled "Chord Progressions for Modern Worship," which is coming soon. The book contains dozens and dozens of basic chord progressions and motifs that can be used to play hundreds of sacred songs in both the PWM and CCM genres. As you learn various worship songs, let those songs serve as a personal occasion for you to draw closer to God and to worship Him with other Believers in the spirit of oneness.

For review, explain the following key words and terms:

- Canticle

- Contemporary Christian Music

- Genre

- Praise & Worship Music

5. Balance Your Music

When performing worship music in public, be sure to balance your music. In other words, do a variety of worship music so that others too can participate in worshipping and honoring God. In public, it's not just about your vertical relationship and personal desire to please God, but it's also about other people's vertical relationship with God and their desire to please Him. That means there's no conflict of interest as long as the focus of the musicians and audience alike is on pleasing God. (Check out the worship song "Please Him" on our ministry homepage: faithchurchofglenville.org.)

Now, just like there are certain kinds of music that help you get into a mood of worship and admiration toward God, there are other kinds of music that help others get into a mood of worship and admiration toward Him. Remember, the second greatest commandment is to "love your neighbor as yourself" (Mark 12:31). So, think about how you would want to be treated when you're in the audience and someone else is leading worship. Would you want to hear music that only the person leading worship enjoyed? Would you want everyone else's musical tastes to be ignored? No, I'm sure.

If you want others to musically participate with you in a public worship experience, be sure to consider the ages, demographics and musical backgrounds of the people in the audience. God is love, and love includes preferring others before ourselves (Romans 12:10). This does not mean that you totally abandon your musical tastes, and it certainly doesn't mean that you neglect to first and foremost follow the leading of God's Spirit. Rather, it means taking time to make sure that the worship experience encourages group participation, so that everyone can enjoy a rich and wonderful time in the presence of God.

Incidentally, this is one of the reasons that private music worship time at home is important. During those personal times, you don't have to consider anyone's musical preferences but your own. Don't neglect your private music worship time with God. Then you won't feel the pressure in public to make the worship experience all about your musical tastes only.

Never disrespect or poke fun at the musical preferences of seniors. There's nothing wrong with good tradition, so don't be condescending when playing hymns, spirituals or any song that is God centered. God never goes out of style, and His power has no expiration date! So when seniors worship Him through "traditional" music, like *Amazing Grace*, it's not about style at all. Rather, it is about having history and relationship with God, reminiscing on the ups and downs they've been through in life, the good times and the bad, and praising God for how He brought them through it all!

If you are young now, then just keep on living. One day you too will be a senior with musical experiences and tastes that span decades. In that day, you won't want your brand of worship music to be ignored, sneered at or joked about. That wouldn't be good then, and it's not good now.

Balance your music. Learn more than one style and genre. This will help equip you to lead audiences in a more holistic musical experience.

6. Publishing History

Worship and love songs are among the most famous and widely published music in the world, dating back centuries. Just consider the songbooks of Psalms (hymns, songs of praise, etc.) and Song of Solomon (ancient love songs). Both of these songbooks were first published in the Bible. And how many copies of the Bible have been published? Over 6 billion copies! This makes the music of the Psalms and the Song of Solomon the most published music lyrics in the world.

Granted, as with nearly all music written 3000 years ago, the melodies were primarily passed from one generation to the next through oral tradition, so no sheet music with the original melodies exist. However, oral transmission of these melodies is still commonplace in churches throughout the world, and the lyrics can be read in any number of Bible translations. Therefore, if you're looking to make a lasting impact in music, writing worship songs and love songs is the best place to start. (Love songs are covered in detail in Part 2: Music entertainment)

For now, remember to avoid writing and performing music that's unworthy of being passed down from one generation to the next. That doesn't mean your music can't be edgy or deal with provocative subjects or controversial matters pertaining to life. You should certainly write about those things if that's your artistic flow and where your interests lie. Just make sure that in the end you are enriching people's lives and not simply making more "junk music" in hopes of selling a few more downloads or getting a few more views or clicks. Do all things in love to the glory of God (1 Corinthians 16:14).

7. God Affirms and Qualifies

Focusing on God and His affirmation of you is where music worship begins and ends. For this reason, be careful about how much human affirmation you seek concerning your music. It's okay to want to make a difference in people's lives through your worship music, and to have your efforts positively reinforced by human means. But don't let it go too far. Remember, God is the One who ultimately qualifies you. This doesn't mean you don't need human tutors to encourage you in your learning. Of course you do. To be sure, you should do everything you can to improve your learning and to gain the approval and affirmation of worthy teachers who have devoted themselves to helping you get better. But as you further your studies, remember that it is God who is most responsible for making you who you are. Your life and abilities are in His hands. He is the One who sustains you.

Regardless of how many times you make a mistake, get discouraged, or want to give up, know that your music purpose is bigger than you. Know that God has gifted you, and in turn called you to do something with that gift. And since He called you, He is well able to affirm and qualify you.

8. Private Performance

Learn to perform for God in private. Play, sing, and write songs to the Lord. Don't be shy. Let Him hear you! Perform your songs for Him anytime of the day. Perform for Him with a sincere heart, one full of love and compassion. Don't worry. God will never laugh at your performance. He's a proud Father! He loves you! And He'd give anything for you, and indeed He has. (Jesus is proof of that.) So don't hold back. Sing melodies to Him. No song is too short or insignificant. No note is too simple. He's listening. Give Him your best in private. That way you don't have to fake it or put on a show for God in public. Your worship will be real!

9. Two Way Street

Since we're on the subject of music worship, a question comes to mind that people often ask me. Should musicians be paid to work in music ministry? Yes, if they have the right skills and attitude about ministry. The Bible says, "the worker deserves his wages" (1 Timothy 5:18). That means good workers deserve to be paid. But musicians who take the "hired hand" approach, and don't care anything about the ministry but only about the money, should be avoided. Jesus said *"The hired hand runs away because he is merely hired and has no real concern for the sheep"* (John 10:14, NLT). Musicians who take that attitude are wrong for music worship in the church, and equally wrong for music entertainment in popular culture. People who care only about money will not likely care much for people. And that kind of attitude is unhealthy.

The truth is the majority of music ministries believe that some form of compensation is necessary for qualified musicians who provide worship music for gatherings. Few will argue that a professional musician should play for free. (For people who believe that musicians should play for free, try going to their jobs and telling their boss that. Then let's see how much they like not getting a check!)

At any rate, every so often you'll run into churches and ministries that believe musicians should be paid with a chicken dinner. I know this for sure because I've met some of them! Listen. Love is a two way street. Ministries that demand excellence in musicianship should also pay with excellence.

Lastly, musicians should strive to be good and faithful in all that they do. Being a good musician but not a faithful musician is not what God wants, nor is it what people want. On the other hand, some musicians are very faithful, but they aren't very good at doing music. This is not good either; however, it is better to have a musician that is faithful, because if a musician is faithful he or she will eventually become good, with enough practice. Faithful practice will lead to improvement. And continued improvement will lead to becoming good. Make no mistake about this: God wants us to be both good and faithful (Matthew 25:20-21).

Offer your best service to God and people in all that you do. Serve people as if you are working for God, because in fact you *are* working for God. If you accept a job assignment playing for a church, don't leave that church for another church down the street just because they offer you a few more bucks per week. If you do, that makes you a hireling, a real hired hand. And if a church dumps you for another musician, when in fact you've been good and faithful to the church, then let them. They don't deserve your services. Ministries that don't honor people who've been good and faithful don't deserve to have people who are good and faithful.

Therefore, the message to musicians is this:

> Don't treat God's church like a gig or a hustle. And stop showing up late to rehearsals and services, for goodness sake. God's work is serious business, and it is a loving business. If you want to know more about God's love, please take some time to seek the Lord, and get to know Him. You'll find that He is the most loving being in the universe, even willing to give up His only Son for you and me. That's real love! But please don't mistake God for a fool. He

is—to quote Dr. Dre, "A murderer's monster." That's right, I said it! God is not some 3-year old child to be toyed with. He is Lord of the universe, able to destroy both body and soul (Matthew 10:28). That's what I call dead! Satan and all of those who have rejected God's salvation will soon find out how terrifying God can be. But as for me, I plan to serve God by serving others, and to treat the work of God with reverence and respect.

And to church ministries and their team members the message is this:

Treat musicians and ministry team members the same way you want to be treated. Don't cut short a musician's paycheck just because he or she decided *not* to have choir rehearsal on Christmas. On Christmas? For real? Deducting from a musician's pay for frivolous reasons is childish. If money is tight and budget cuts are needed, fine. Just say that. But don't go around looking for reasons to unjustly dock a person's pay! If you treat musicians like hirelings instead of ministry team members, don't blame them for acting like hirelings!

Let's all do our best to grow in grace, work together and walk in Christian love. Let's all approach God's work with humility, thanksgiving, and mutual respect for one another. This is the way to address the servant who is worthy of his or her hire (1 Timothy 5:18).

10. Investing in Music

The Bible says, "*Where your treasure is, there will your heart be also*" (Matthew 6:21 KJV). Put another way, churches that have a heart for excellence in music ministry will indeed invest time and resources in musicians, instruments and sound equipment. Churches that don't treasure music will usually spend zero dollars on it. These are often the same churches that complain about not having a good musician.

One can easily discover how important music is to a congregation by checking their music ministry budget. Even churches with very little money should at least be able to afford to enroll some of their youth in private music lessons, which is not expensive at all. And if the church has no youth, that is all the more reason to offer free music lessons to children in the neighborhood. So there's no excuse for any church not to invest money in music ministry especially since music is so important in today's youth culture.

Don't misunderstand. The primary mission of the church is to evangelize. However, a fully equipped music ministry under the direction of a qualified, spirit-filled music minster can play an important role in evangelizing. For starters, a musician can help set the atmosphere so that the spoken Word is more easily administered. Secondly, a musician can minister songs that are lyrically packed with the Word of God. That makes the music a conduit through which God can flow, permeating the minds and hearts of people.

Now I know this may be hard for some of us preachers to admit, because some of us think that God can only move through the Spoken Word. But that's not true. God can move however He wants to, whenever He wants to, and through whomever He wants to! He's God. He's been known to speak through a burning bush (Exodus 3:4), a still small voice (1 Kings 19:11-13) and even through a donkey (Numbers 22:28). In fact, David—one of the most famous biblical musicians ever—drove out evil spirits through the use of music (1 Samuel 16:23). He had a deep, rich love for God and was so spirit-filled that the presence of God flowed out of him and through his music. This in no way negates the preeminence of the preached Word. I'm just saying that God cannot be boxed in.

Never forget that God can touch people through whatever medium He chooses. This is why investing in music ministry can be so beneficial. Music is a powerful medium. And since it plays such an important role in today's youth culture, it is in most churches' best interests to have a thriving music and arts ministry. This will not just happen by itself; ministry leaders and musicians will need to work together to prayerfully map out an investment plan for the music ministry. There will of course be costs associated with doing so, but investing in people first, and equipment second, is what music ministry is all about. Never forget, the most valuable commodity in ministry is people. Jesus didn't die for music or sound equipment. He died for people. And if a person can use music as a tool to soften the hearts of unbelievers, then by all means we should invest in music so that more people can be reached.

11. Multiple Revenue Streams

The Bible teaches that we should wisely spread out our wealth and diversify our investments, so not to put all of our resources into one "basket" (Ecclesiastes 11:1-2). In doing so, musicians, especially Ministers of Music who have multiple revenue streams, can be of greater help to the cause of Christ and the local church. If musicians diversify, using their gifts and talents to create more than one source of revenue, they wouldn't need to ask for top dollar from their home churches, nor would they have to play at five different churches every Sunday just to make ends meet!

Please, don't get me wrong. There is nothing wrong with playing at more than one church as long as 1) you believe it's the Lord's will for you to do so, 2) you do an excellent job at each church and are faithful, and 3) you don't wear yourself out in the process! Having multiple revenue streams is good for musicians, and such will allow musicians to grow their wealth and better support the work of Christ financially.

Case in point, many years ago I played for a small church in which my yearly tithes were more than the yearly salary the church paid me. The reason I was able to give more money than I received is because I had other revenue streams, including a lucrative job as a music producer and arranger for a very famous music entertainer. This other source of income allowed me to make far more money than my local church could afford to pay me. In turn, I gave monetarily more than I received from them.

In conclusion, diversify your investments and maximize each of your God-given talents and gifts. Don't put all your "eggs" or resources into one basket. Having multiple revenue streams will empower you to be of greater service to your family, church and community.

12. Respecting the Home Front

So what do you do? You have a steady job in town playing for a church or group. You're playing weddings and other gigs and everything is going great. But you get a call to do a couple of dates out of town, perhaps a mini tour. Tough, right? You don't want to damage things on the home front (i.e. serving at church, doing gigs, teaching, etc.) because you are committed and that is your bread and butter when it comes to making steady money. But at the same time you also have a desire to take advantage of other great opportunities that come your way. It's not that those opportunities are better or more important than your home front, rather it's that you're not a one-dimensional musician or artist and you want to do other things as well. So, how do you handle the home front when these opportunities arise?

First and foremost, keep your word. Walk in integrity. I cannot stress this enough. As I mentioned before, the Bible says

"Choose a good reputation over great riches; being held in high esteem is better than silver or gold" (Proverbs 22:1, NLT). If you have committed yourself to a church, band, group, director, concert promoter, businessperson, club owner or restaurateur then keep your word! Don't renege on your word, obligations or commitments just because another opportunity has opened up for you. But that doesn't mean you should pass up a good opportunity, so long as you have a proper replacement to cover for you.

Secondly, if, for example, you have a standing obligation to a church or some other organization or person, contact them as soon as possible to see if they will agree to let you find a competent substitute or fill-in. If they agree to that, then it's your responsibility to make sure that:

a) The substitute is musically excellent and known for being ON TIME.

b) There is no "bad blood" between the substitute and the church or artist for which he/she will be filling in.

c) You let the artist or church know well in advance who it is that you want to fill in, so that they can voice their approval or disapproval of the person.

d) The substitute has his or her own transportation, instrument(s), equipment, and necessary attire to do the primary job, as well as any necessary rehearsals.

e) The terms of remuneration (i.e. payment) are in writing, and that all parties involved are agreed so that there are no misunderstandings as to how much will be paid, when will it be paid, and whether it will be cash, check, money order or electronic payment via PayPal or bank wire transfer, etc.

That you may have to miss work every now and then is something you should seriously consider whenever you make long-term commitments on the home front. Therefore, be sure you have the option to bring in a substitute musician or group whenever signing an agreement with a church, organization or individual. And don't abuse that option. Use it only when necessary, otherwise you will get a reputation for canceling dates.

Having given proper notice, you should definitely take advantage of exceptional opportunities that come your way, so long as you honor your written agreements and do not damage your good name. Also, be prayerful and extra sensitive when it comes to missing your weekly church service for other opportunities that arise. Remember, the Word says "Seek the Kingdom of God above all else, and live righteously, and he will give you everything you need" (Matthew 6:33, NLT).

Faith, which is a community choir I lead, does a gospel concert once a month in Cleveland, Ohio for Live Nation Entertainment (Live Nation Entertainment is a billion dollar company formed from the merger of Live Nation and Ticketmaster in 2010.) The concert we do is downtown on Sunday morning, once a month, and is geared toward a multicultural crowd. Because Faith is a community choir, many of the singers and musicians involved have to miss their Sunday service, once a month, in order to participate. The members of Faith all get permission from their pastors to participate, and count it a great opportunity to minister music to an audience of both believers and non-believers. For those who participate, it is worth missing only one Sunday a month because of the greater good of reaching out to those who do not know Christ. But again, each member of Faith has been given permission from his or her pastor or ministry leader to participate. It's the right thing to do.

If you honor God first, and handle your personal and professional business with prudence and integrity, God will cause awesome opportunities to come your way and you will prosper greatly. You reap what you sow. Therefore, keep God first in all that you do. I know that there are some ministry leaders and Christian artists who may unfairly demand too much of your time. Some may even imply that you shouldn't work with other people or ministries outside of theirs or outside of your home church. Worse, there are some who may openly try to force you or guilt you into turning down other great musical opportunities that come your way. They might go as far as claiming that God will not bless you if you take outside opportunities. Sometimes their advice is right, and you should pass on certain "outside" opportunities that may not be good for you. And other times their advice may be wrong. But you win, either way, even if a ministry leader unfairly squashes an opportunity for you and tells you that you can't go. Why? Because God has your back! And you will never lose when it comes to honoring God with your gifts and talents, even if a ministry leader or artist happens to make a bad call and overstep his or her place regarding what you should or should not do. So obey your pastor or ministry leader. They're not perfect. And guess what? Neither are you. We must all learn to honor the ministry leaders under whom we serve or the Christian artists or organizations for whom we work. With prayer, you will find the proper balance for handling other opportunities that come up.

Be sure to make a valiant effort to attend your main weekly church service, and especially Bible study, because faith is developed by hearing the Word (Romans 10:17) and putting it into practice (James 2:14-26). Honor your Home Front musical commitments, sacred and secular. Be a person of your word, a person of integrity, and a student of *the* Word.

13. Don't Forget Your Hymns

The Greek word *hymnos* means a song of praise, which is where we get the word hymn. The Bible contains many songs of praise (hymns), especially in the book of Psalms. Jesus said, "Everything must be fulfilled that is written about me in the Law of Moses, the Prophets and the Psalms" (Luke 24:44, NIV). The book of Psalms contains songs that foretell of Christ, his works, and that offer praise to God. Indeed, Psalms[1] is the Bible's hymnal of praise and worship music, and it has been around for over 3000 years.

Songs that are rich in scripture and biblical doctrine are important to the modern repertoire of contemporary praise and worship music, and sacred music in general. For this reason, it is important to not become so contemporary-minded in your music that you neglect to incorporate scripturally-based hymns or songs of praise into your worship experience. That doesn't mean your music needs to sound dated or out of style. Remember, worship music is not about a date or a style, because God has no date; neither can He be confined to a particular style. But your music should be well rounded, so that more and more people may be drawn to Christ through the biblical message contained in your music.

Additionally, you can even write a hymn yourself. Yes you! Hymns are not exclusive to dead songwriters, but exclusive to God. Who do you think inspired David to write the hymn of comfort that says *"The LORD is my shepherd; I have everything I need. He lets me rest in green meadows; he leads me beside peaceful streams. He renews my strength. He guides me along right paths, bringing honor to his name. Even when I walk through the dark valley of death, I*

---

1 *Israel's ancient collection of praise and worship songs* (Unger's Bible Dictionary)

will not be afraid, for you are close beside me. Your rod and your staff protect and comfort me. You prepare a feast for me in the presence of my enemies. You welcome me as a guest, anointing my head with oil. My cup overflows with blessings. Surely your goodness and unfailing love will pursue me all the days of my life, and I will live in the house of the LORD forever" (Psalm 23:1-24, NLT). It was God of course who inspired this hymn.

Keep in mind that when you walk with God He will give you spiritual songs, songs of comfort, songs of praise, encouragement and worship. He will inspire you to write music that will uplift people and encourage their faith in God. So take the time to read the Psalms. It's full of songs that have impacted the world, even more than the music of The Beatles! If you're a serious musician, singer, or songwriter, it only makes sense to study the top musicians, singers, and songwriters of all time. And those songwriters and producers can be found in the book of Psalms.

The writers and musicians of the Psalms were music artists of the highest order. Their music has stood the test of time because it was God inspired and not written based on talent alone. Do you want your music to last for centuries? Study the book of Psalms. Do you want your performances (sacred or secular) to have a lasting impact on audiences? Study the book of Psalms. In it you will find songs of praise and adoration to God, and you will discover the principles of personal worship and devotion towards Him. Such will sure up your spiritual base and serve as a catalyst for you to do any kind of music.

14. Royal Etiquette

There is a way to treat royalty. For instance, regardless of how one may feel about the President of the United States, the office deserves a certain amount of respect in a civilized society. The same can be said for the Queen of England or the Prime Minister of France. If, however, a king or queen of a nation should be honored, and his or her office respected, how much more should we honor God, who is the King of Kings, and who created all things?

Some people, because of lack of knowledge, do not properly reverence God or His presence. For many people it is not their fault, as no one taught them what to do when God (i.e. His presence) shows up in a service or worship experience.

First, there is no "one" way to reverence God. In fact, there are many. Moses, for instance, took off His shoes when he came near the presence of God, because God told Him not to "come any closer" with his shoes on (Exodus 3:5-6). In another case, God required others to consecrate themselves (i.e. go without food or fast for a time and give up other conveniences) before they could handle the sacred ark, which was a symbol of the presence of God (1 Chronicles 15:14).

Whatever the case may be, you should always show respect to God by entering His presence with thanksgiving and praise (Psalm 100:4; 34:3). To come into a church service and merely sit in your seat with your arms or legs crossed (like you're doing God a favor to be there) is a flagrant disregard for the presence of God, and a defiant show of disrespect. Never sit during praise and worship in church or otherwise act unengaged during a worship experience or gathering of believers. The air you're breathing right now belongs to God! So, show a little respect.

Royal etiquette should always be practiced, if you're going to maintain a healthy relationship with God. And all believers should share these principles of respect with the next generation, so that they will know what it means to honor God in their heart, and to praise Him openly and unashamedly for His unmerited favor and love.

How we reverence God will vary depending on the nation and culture familiar to us. But all believers, no matter what nation we are from, should show reverence to God and demonstrate respect for Him in a tangible way at all times.

Notes

Part 2

Music Entertainment

1. The Horizontal

The second of only three things you can do with music is to entertain with it. Indeed, music entertainment is a wonderful invention that works best when it is done with integrity. Make no mistake. The greatest problem in music entertainment today is the lack of integrity in songs and music that claim "artistic expression" as a license to say anything and do anything. And here is the reason why you should never fall for that lie. You are not a bastard. Let me say it again. You are not a bastard, which is the reason it's not okay for you to say anything or do anything you want, under the guise of artistic expression. A bastard is an illegitimate child who doesn't have a father that lays claim to him or her. Well… you are not illegitimate! According to the Bible, you have a Father who lays claim to you! His name is Jehovah! He is the Creator of all things, and you and I are accountable to Him. So, it's not okay to say or do anything you want, and step back and say, "it's just music" or "it's just art," as if that's an excuse. Stop it! Doing art is not a license to kill. And trust me. Bad art kills! It helps destroy the moral fabric of our culture, turning young musicians and artists into ditto heads and zombies with no respect for God or each other. Don't you realize how much God, our Father, loves us? That's why He has rules. The Bible says, "the one who loves their children is careful to discipline them" (Proverbs 13:24). No discipline? No love.

Since you have a Father, it means there are instructions and guidelines you must follow, if you want to be successful in music and in life. You are not some abandoned child left to fend for yourself, making up rules as you see fit, and doing any and everything you want with no regard for anyone. Regardless of how perfect or imperfect your childhood may have been, know that God is your Father and that His love for you is a billion times higher that any human being's love for you; higher than even your earthly mother's or father's love.

So, honor God through your musical expression of art and entertainment. Don't dishonor *our* Father over something as small as a song or a scandalous music video. Having worked on music projects involving Tupac, Michael Jackson, Toni Braxton, R-Kelly, Mary J. Blige and many other artists and entertainers I can tell you that the music industry will tempt you to break the rules in an effort to "find your voice" or be "different" or "make more money." Since you have a Father who knows everything, and since He has rules and guidelines for protecting you (guidelines made clear through the study of His Word, the Bible), you have no reason to give into negative temptation. You *can* become an extremely successful music artist and entertainer, without "selling your soul" or becoming someone's puppet.

So, by all means, do music entertainment. Make songs that will serve as a beautiful horizontal expression between people of all ages. Share your music. Write and perform songs about any and every subject you can think of. Just be sure to do it with integrity.

2. Love Songs

There is nothing like a love song that captures the affections between people who love each other. Note the lyrics below, which come from an ancient love song.

(Female): Kiss me and kiss me again, for your love is sweeter than wine. How fragrant your cologne...[2] My lover is like a sachet of myrrh lying between my breasts. He is like a bouquet of sweet henna blossoms from the vineyards of Engedi.[3]

(Male): Your lips are like scarlet ribbon; your mouth is inviting. Your cheeks are like rosy pomegranates behind your veil. Your

---

2 Song of Solomon 1:2, 3
3 Song of Solomon 1:12-14

neck is as beautiful as the tower of David, jeweled with the shields of a thousand heroes. Your breasts are like two fawns, twin fawns of a gazelle grazing among the lilies.[4]

Provocative, right? And those words come straight out of the Bible (Song of Solomon). One thing's for sure. The man in the song (Solomon) was not talking about the *breastplate of righteousness* (Ephesians 6:14) when he mentions the word breast. So please don't try to spiritualize the words. Solomon wasn't trying to be spiritual when he wrote those lyrics. He was trying to be sensual. (And here we thought Marvin Gaye invented sexy singing!)

Listen. There is nothing wrong with romantic music or steamy love songs, just as long as they don't violate biblical rules of love and expediency (1 Corinthians 10:23-24, MSG). I realize that there has been disagreement on the subject of love songs in some religious circles. But the fact is that the provocative song lyrics mentioned above come from the Bible. And those words of poetry didn't get in the Bible by accident, but God put them there.

Also, you should keep in mind that the music in the Song of Solomon expresses romance between a man and his wife, not between strangers or live-in lovers. The song portrays a picture of two people who have made a wholesome and healthy

---

4 Song of Solomon 4:3-5

commitment to God and to each other to live in holy matrimony as husband and wife, to love each other, respect each other and cherish each other.

But don't misunderstand. Solomon was *far* from being a perfect man, perfect husband or perfect dad, but the passion he shares with his wife through his poetry and sultry songwriting is to be admired and enjoyed. So, enjoy his songs! And write or perform your own love songs, if you choose. Do your music with integrity and it will make for good, healthy music entertainment.

3. An Opportunity

In music entertainment, you have a wonderful opportunity to impact many lives for the better. The music industry can be savage at times, but you can help make a difference by being in top form musically and spiritually. Don't forget that if your music skills are weak due to laziness and a refusal to practice your instrument, then it weakens your effectiveness as a musician and artist.

David, one of the most famous musicians in the Bible, rose to fame quickly. He was a musician and a solder, and he used his skills in those areas to achieve great success. His gifts as a musician and a skilled warrior opened many doors for him, and he practiced his instrument—the lyre, becoming highly skilled. David was a very effective music artist who practiced a lot. You too should practice a lot!

David was also known for being good looking and having the spirit of God in his life (1 Samuel 16:18), which is why you should never go out of the house with your pants sagging or your dress looking like a hoochie! That means when you go out to perform you look your best. There's nothing wrong with jeans and a t-shirt. But God also made other clothes as well, and you should try them sometime. Perhaps a nice modern suit or dress wouldn't hurt. Most importantly, wear a smile on your face and carry an attitude that is Christ-like.

As a music entertainer you may have opportunities to meet kings and queens, presidents and prime ministers, the rich and famous. You, like David, can develop meaningful personal relationships with all types of people in the industry and become a force in the business. You might also, at the appropriate time, point others to a better life; a life of love and happiness in Christ. You do this not by being "preachy" or weird or always talking about God or the Bible every two seconds! No, you do this by demonstrating excellence, neighborly-love, equity and justice in all that you do. You do this by not compromising your spirituality, musicality or integrity. Don't make cheap, trashy songs with very little musical value. Aim for excellence, and maintain your "bearings" and your integrity in all things (1 Corinthians 9:19-23).

It's true that not everyone is cut out to work in some of the darker corners of music entertainment. There are places that even I won't go. But there are plenty of other places you *can* go and have a positive impact, so do it. Be a living example of Christ in music.

4. Get Wisdom!

Every musician, singer and songwriter should read the book of Proverbs at least once every year. With the help of electronic Bible apps you can listen to the entire book in one sitting, so there is no excuse not to do it.

The book of Proverbs is a book of wisdom that will help you make the best decisions in life. It will teach you how to become a critical thinker, how to use discretion in making decisions, and how to become the consummate professional musician/artist you were purposed to be. Studying Proverbs (and doing what it says) is the key to you becoming a wise person, the key to you gaining wisdom. Wisdom, which comes from God, will help protect you from the heightened greed, sexuality and arrogance that negatively impact people from all walks of life in the secular and sacred world of music. In a culture where many popular songs and music videos are all about about money, bragging, sex and violence, wisdom will be the factor that makes the difference in your life, distinguishing you from other artists.

By wisdom God "laid the earth's foundations" and by understanding "he set the heavens in place" (Proverbs 3:19). God is the Maker of wisdom, and true wisdom is to obey God, to love what He loves and to hate what He hates. Wisdom is allowing the mindset that Jesus had—a mindset of love and self sacrifice—to be in you, and to think like Jesus thought (Philippians 2:5). If you pray and ask God for wisdom, He will give it to you and you will begin to think like God thinks, and act like God acts. No, it won't make you "God." Rather, it will teach you how to obey God. And if you obey God, then you will truly be wise!

Please don't miss the point here, otherwise you might come to a very bad end. Get wisdom and understanding, no matter the cost. They will guard your life and help you avoid the pain and regret that inevitably come with a life where there is no accountability. Superstar artists are often told that their "mess" doesn't stink. But it does! So, don't fall for that. Listen to your parents and/or a trusted guardian. Find a good pastor who is faithful to God and honest toward people; someone who has your back and to whom you can be accountable, a person who will lovingly tell you when you're wrong, and make it his or her business to always point you to the Bible as the ultimate authority on how you should live—not a person who points to his or herself as *the* authority. (Be picky about a pastor, but remember pastors are not perfect, and neither are you!)

Through your study and application of the Word of God, you will grow in wisdom and knowledge. That wisdom will help you avoid the greed, gossip, abuse, egotism, deceit, malice, slander, addictions, disrespect, lust, lies and other pitfalls you are bound to face in the music world. Best of all, wisdom will be a lifelong companion that will help ornament your life at all times and in all places. Get wisdom!

5. Staying Power

Staying power is another way of expressing longevity in the music business. Longevity is something you want. The alternative would be becoming a one-hit wonder. And trust me, you don't want to be a one-hit wonder (i.e. someone who makes only one good song his or her entire career).

You can experience a long and successful life in music without "selling out" or being untrue to your musical tastes. Selling out, in this context, means trying to musically be someone you're not, in order to get ahead. You should never do that, but always be yourself. That doesn't mean you shouldn't learn from other great musicians and artists. On the contrary, you should be a musical sponge that sops up every good piece of music you come in contact with. This is important because longevity requires that you reinvent yourself and not become stagnated or stuck in one mode or style of music for the rest of your life. You can be true to yourself and still grow and evolve musically. That's what true longevity is about.

Keep learning from others who've been successful entertainers. Don't just check out current artists on the charts. Go back and learn from the greats. Study the lives and careers of music artists from all genres, including jazz, rock, country, bluegrass, gospel, classical, R&B, rap, and alternative styles of music. Study music of the 1400s, 1500s, and all the way through today's music. Study world music, which is, in my view, the same as saying study *all* music. Study the lives of successful musicians in the Bible, like Jubal, David, Asaph, Miriam and others who were exceptional composers and music leaders (Exodus 15: 20-21). Learn from the successes and failures of musicians and artists throughout history. Learn, learn, learn!

If you become a student of the Word of God, and prayerfully glean from the lives of other people, you will learn what to do and what not to do in music. And ultimately with God's help you can establish your own brand of music and build a career that will last for decades to come.

6. Content Management

Whether performing music for worship or entertainment purposes, it is important that the content of your songs be based on trusted truths. That doesn't mean you shouldn't explore fictional subject matters in your music. On the contrary, be brave and fearless in composing all types of music. Don't limit yourself. Just be sure that in the end you avoid portraying half-truths as fact, much less complete falsehoods as being real.

Avoid making music in a way that glorifies violence, encourages unhealthy sexual behavior or promotes lies and hateful stereotypes that can be harmful to listeners. Today, many good songs have been ruined by the unnecessary addition of explicit lyrics, nonsensical content, and distasteful images in music videos masquerading as marketing ploys. And for what? A few more downloads or views? Is the sale of your integrity worth getting a few more concert dates or even a Grammy nomination? No, it isn't.

Listen. Don't become a musical prostitute for sale to the highest bidder. Christ died for you! That's how important you are, no matter how sordid your past may be. Demonstrate your gratefulness by being original and innovative in your music, but without spreading lies and misery. You can tell a story about violence without displaying violent images on screen. And you can musically arouse the romantic instincts of listeners without relying on trashy sexuality. Don't give into agents, producers or executives who encourage you to compromise your honesty for the sake of popularity or a few more dollars. It is not worth it.

Make a choice to fill your mind with things that are "honorable, right, pure, lovely and admirable" (Philippians 4:8). For whatever is in your heart will come out in your music.

7. Promotion

Promoting your music will take time, diligence, and hard work. The beautiful thing is that you have a God-given purpose, so your success is assured as long as you stay in God's will. Stay true to your music convictions while taking care to build your listening audience. Find those who celebrate your music and not merely tolerate it. If you do so correctly, you'll be promoted in due time. Don't despise putting in extra work to excel. Getting ahead requires a certain amount of groundwork to be laid first. It takes time to establish a firm music foundation. The deeper the foundation is, the higher your musical heights. The higher the musical heights are, the more integrity necessary for you to properly maintain those heights.

Finally, the more integrity you develop, the less likely you are to make unwise decisions that can cause a downfall in your life overnight. As was mentioned earlier, many famous performers have had very public downfalls because somewhere along the way they neglected to keep God first. Don't criticize their failures. Pray for them. But please avoid repeating their mistakes.

Promotion comes from God (Psalms 75:6), so be patient while God perfects your inner character. He will promote you at the right time. (Learn the song "Promotion" from the Lafayette Carthon YouTube Channel.)

8. Compliments and Criticism

When your music is criticized, take it with a grain of salt. The same goes for compliments about your music. It's important to not take as 100% true or false what people say about you, whether good or bad. The truth will usually fall somewhere in the middle.

When you receive rave reviews for a good performance, be thankful. But do not read too much into it. The same people who are singing your praises this week may be booing you off stage next week. People are fickle. One minute, they can't get enough of you. The next minute, they claim they were never into you. So, be careful and stay open to constructive criticism because it's healthy for you. But do not take things too personally.

Never let anyone's opinion of you or your music compare to what the God says about you and your music. He has the final word.

9. Recap: Perfecting Music Entertainment

To conclude this section, let's recap three important principles that are helpful in perfecting music entertainment. 1) You should consult daily with the Music Maker for cutting edge musical ideas. 2) Do not neglect your personal music tastes. 3) Continue learning how to better *serve* your audience.

Consult With the Music Maker

A single music idea from the Maker of Music (God) can lead to massive musical success beyond your wildest dreams. It can lead to new and innovative ideas never before thought of. If you consult with God, He is more than able to give you clarity and insight on cutting edge artistic ideas that you could never get anywhere else.

From fresh ideas involving new music concepts and groundbreaking songs to new products and platforms, God can give you witty inventions never before imagined. Whether it pertains to new products on the music side or cutting-edge technologies in other industries, even healthcare, God can pour into your mind ideas that can positively impact the lives of millions and even billions of people. For God controls all industries, including music entertainment. In fact, "the earth is the Lord's, and everything in it" (Psalm 24:1). He is the CEO or CEOs. He ultimately controls the Internet, television, radio, and all forms of media. Best of all, He knows the way you should go. So keep your eyes on Him. Consult with Him. And He will help you to become a healthier, wealthier and more artistic you!

Don't Neglect Your Personal Music Tastes

Don't neglect your own musical tastes when writing or performing your original compositions or simply listening to music. Be sure to put "you" in your music. Expand your musical palate (i.e. taste) by sampling all types of music, from neo-soul to even Peking opera! Everything God made is good, so there's no such thing as bad music, only people who do music in a bad way.

Learn to Serve Your Audience

A lot of people don't like the word serve, but if you want to get ahead in music entertainment, learn how to better serve your audience. The greatest person in God's Kingdom is the servant (Matthew 18:1-5). So, don't avoid serving. Rather, embrace it. Continue to sharpen the way in which you oblige your audience, but without compromising your musical veracity. I know I said this before but it bears repeating. Do your research and change with the times, where appropriate. People are constantly changing.

Don't be arrogant and take the kind of attitude that says, "I'm not gonna change my music at all, because my style is unique, fresh and different; and if people can't get with this freshness, forget them!" That's the wrong attitude. Great artists know how to reinvent themselves, in order to remain relevant. They don't thumb their noses up at their listening audience, but are able to find the balance in remaining true to their musical convictions and pleasing their audience. They're able to balance the two. So, keep a healthy, equitable servant's attitude when it comes to the music you create for your audience.

Notes

Part 3

Music Teaching

1. Making Musicians

Music teaching is the third of only three things you can do with music. There is, however, a reason that music teaching is third and final. It is because teaching is the most impactful thing you can do with music. And when a person teaches music correctly, it can impact thousands, even millions of people. On the other hand, when a person teaches music *incorrectly*, he or she can also negatively impact hundreds of thousands of people, and even millions of people!

To duplicate one's efforts is one of the underlining principles of music teaching. To take the good that you know and to instill that in others, while helping others to excel beyond what you've achieved, is what great teaching is all about. Two is better than one. And three is better still. Two excellently trained musicians is a good thing, but three excellently trained musicians are even better. So duplicating yourself in others is better than keeping valuable knowledge to yourself and never passing it on.

Don't die having never shared with anyone the important music lessons and life lessons you've learned. Instead, give back by doing the following:

- Devote your life to learning—first about God, then about everything else.

- Find key teachers who can guide you. Joshua was a phenomenal leader in the Bible (read the book of Joshua). But he had a phenomenal teacher, Moses (read the book of Exodus). Mother Jeanette Steele was my early childhood piano teacher. She introduced me to the music of Beethoven and Debussy. Later, my choral music teacher was Dr. William Woods. He introduced me to the music of Art Tatum and Oscar Peterson. Good music teachers are "pointers." They point you in the way you should go (Proverbs 22:6).

- Be generous in sharing what you've learned with others, for you reap what you sow (Galatians 6:7). If you are stingy with your knowledge, others will be stingy with you. That doesn't mean you shouldn't be paid for your knowledge. But if you share valuable knowledge, God will cause others to share valuable knowledge with you.

2. Honor Your Teachers

As I mentioned earlier, the late Mother Jeanette Steele and Dr. William Woods were my childhood teachers. I have made it a point to honor them, and you too should honor your teachers. Take care to never scoff at your teachers, and never belittle the teaching profession, no matter how smart or successful you become. I know there's an old saying, "Those who can't do, teach." But that is one of the most ignorant statements ever spoken. Because teaching music *correctly* is such a high call, it's important to respect that call. So respect it! And respect those who guide you toward the most important principles of music, the first principle being to love God with all your heart, soul, body, mind and resources (Luke 10:27; Proverbs 3:9; Malachi 3:10). That is the first principle in life and in music.

Always remember that the single greatest tragedy in music history, which we know of, occurred when the artist formally known as Lucifer dishonored his teacher, God. Pun intended! (Isaiah 14:12-15; Luke 10:17-20). Lucifer, now called Satan, dishonored God by letting his talent go to his head. It was God who gave Lucifer his music talent. It was God who gifted him. But that wasn't enough for Lucifer. Lucifer wanted to be completely in charge of all of heaven, even in charge of God! His arrogance blinded him and caused him to become embattled with God. That's crazy! You can't beat God! God made everything, including Lucifer. So there was only one way that battle was going to end. God: 1 Lucifer: 0

Lucifer made a fatal mistake in refusing to honor his Maker and Teacher, God—the ultimate teacher of the universe. As a result, he fell from grace, lost his name, his title and position, and ruined his entire life, not to mention the lives of the other angels who joined him in his rebellion. Don't let that happen to you. Don't dishonor God, and don't dishonor those He has placed in your life to teach you. To dishonor them is to dishonor God, just like to dishonor your parents or guardians is to dishonor God.

Be careful not to become an arrogant know-it-all, no matter how phenomenal you become as a musician and artist. You didn't become who you are by yourself. You had help, God's help! So, take time, where appropriate, to honor those who have helped you to properly develop. Take time to honor your teachers. And of course always honor God, putting Him first in all that you do.

3. A Gift to Teach

Successful musicians and artists sometimes make excellent teachers, but sometimes they do not. The reason has to do with one's musical purpose and skillset. Some artists and musicians are destined to teach. It's what they were born to do. Others are musical virtuosos with unusual technical skills and abilities, but not necessarily cut out for teaching. Some teachers are cut out to work with particular types of students, as in working with beginner students or intermediate students. Other teachers with high technical ability and knowledge prefer to teach only the highest performing students.

In reality, the world needs all types of teachers. Not all teachers are cut out to work with 3-year olds. It takes a special kind of patience. And not all teachers have the technical prowess to mentor jazz virtuosos like Jacob Collier or classical virtuosos like Yuja Wang (check out Yuja's performance of *Flight of the Bumblebee*.)

But don't misunderstand. Some of the best teachers are not necessarily virtuosos. In fact, some of the best music teachers are the best, not because of their playing, but because of their mastery in the art of sequential learning. In other words, they know how to take students, step-by-step, through the process of becoming outstanding performers.

Take Nadia Boulanger, for instance. Though her name may not be familiar to some, Ms. Boulanger was a mentor to some of the most notable musicians and composers in modern history, including Aaron Copland, Quincy Jones, Philip Glass, Elliott Carter, Virgil Thompson, and Marc Blitzstein—just to name a few. She personally thought very little of herself as a composer, yet she was instrumental in the development of some of the greatest 20th century composers and musicians of all time. This goes to show that you can have a powerful impact in music as a music teacher, even if you're not considered the best of the best as a musician.

You might also know a teacher of a different profession, Phil Jackson, the former NBA coach of the L.A. Lakers and the Chicago Bulls. Phil Jackson played professional basketball. And though he might not be considered by some to be among the greatest basketball players of all time, he will certainly go down in sports history as one of the most successful coaches of all time, having coached many of the top NBA players, including Michael Jordan and Kobe Bryant. He also holds the record for the head coach with the most NBA championship titles, 11 to be exact. So, some of the best teachers are not necessarily the best players.

The question remains, do you believe God has gifted you to teach music? Do you enjoy finding new ways to break down information, making it easy to understand, and then sharing that information with others? Great! Teaching might be your calling. If so, the thing to do now is to work diligently at becoming the best performer you can be, and to teach others as you yourself learn. Study formally and learn the academics of music. Go to college and major or minor in Music Education, and keep learning as much as you can. And after you are finished learning, learn some more! That's right. Never stop learning, because there's no such thing as being finished learning in life.

Remember that good teachers are, first and foremost, teachable. That means they are learners. Secondly, they are knowledgeable and know how to motivate others to learn. (Note: if you have very little patience, you won't make a good music teacher until that changes.) Good teachers are patient. They take their time and don't yell at students or embarrass students. Good music teachers are accessible and reachable, and they want to answer questions as students make an effort to learn.

Whether you want to teach music privately or publicly or both, it is important to develop an attitude of continuous learning. The more knowledge you take in, the more you can impart to others. But be humble, and not too quick to open your mouth and share, unless you are invited to do so. No one likes a know-it-all. Allow teaching opportunities to come to you by learning to recognize musicians who are reaching out for help and want to learn more.

4. The Money Myth

Contrary to what some might think working-class musicians (as distinct from top selling recording artists) can earn a respectable income, especially those who have a college degree and a passion to teach. For example, a highly skilled private music instructor can earn from $50/hour to $75/hour on average.[5] Add freelance studio work, which can pay upwards of $380 for a three-hour studio session, and a musician can certainly pay some bills.[6] Wedding

---

[5] Based on private lesson rates at the following institutions: 1) University of Missouri Community Music Program http://music.missouri.edu/communityprograms, 2) Nazareth College Community Music Program http://www.naz.edu/dept/cmp/, 3) Lori Moran Music Studio http://lorimoranmusic.com/ratesandpolicies.html

[6] American Federation of Musicians

singers can make $300-$500 just to sing a couple of songs, and successful church choir directors can make on average $39,000 a year or more.[7] In fact, the national average salary for a school music teacher is $60,400 a year.[8]

Musicians make far more money in less time than the average worker. For example, a person making minimum wage in California will earn $1,820 for 182 hours of work. That's at $10 an hour, which is presently the highest minimum wage in America. Now compare that with a musician. For example, in Cleveland, Ohio a low-skilled church musician can make $13,000 for the same 182 hours of work! That's $71 an hour! See the difference? Musicians make far more money in less time than the average person. And the musician who manages his or her money properly can be wealthy in no time at all, if they know what to do and stick to it.

According to the American Guild of Organists the pay scale for a full-time church organist with a Bachelor's Degree is $63,131 - $83,123 a year, $72,368 - $96,632 a year with a Master's Degree and $80,915 - $107,967 a year with a Doctoral Degree (including benefits).[9] Musicians who are not proficient or do not market themselves effectively or have a poor reputation will of course make a lot less, but the potential is there for those who are willing to maximize their talents and receive proper training from successful mentors.

---

7 http://www.payscale.com/research/US/Job=Church_Choir_Director/Salary
8 United States Department of Labor http://www.bls.gov/oes/current/oes251121.htm
9 American Guild of Organists http://www.agohq.org/docs/pdf/salary.pdf

So forget the myth that being a musician is not a real job. It is a real job that can make you more money than the average person. Just be sure to balance your need for financial independence with that of fulfilling your musical purpose.

5. The Degree Myth

To be an excellent music teacher you do not necessarily need a degree. But a degree does help. Understand, if you earn a degree then it means that you are a finisher. Teachers need to be finishers; they need to get things done within a certain timeframe. This points to the principle of why some teachers who don't have a degree can sometimes earn more money than teachers with a degree. In a word, experience. Teachers with experience in getting things done, but who don't have a degree, can be very valuable teachers. Sometimes they can be more valuable than teachers *with* a degree—but not usually.

Don't get hung up on the word "degree." Rather, focus on the word "education." Become a great educator—one who teaches, mentors and helps students grow to maturity in a particular area of study.

6. Actions Teach Louder Than Words

Whether formal or informal, the things you do as a music artist will influence the people around you. Your artistry puts you in a unique position to impact people's thoughts and understanding about music and art. In that sense it makes you a sort of music teacher—an informal one, but one without necessarily the traditional walls of a classroom.

A music teacher of the informal type can be a good thing, but it can also be a bad thing. Many music artists have the tremendous power of a teacher but without the accountability most "real" teachers are subject to. Artists get to say anything they want, do anything they want, and influence tens of thousands of young listeners with their music without anyone telling them "no don't do this" or "no, don't do that." This is problematic because of the emotional instability, chaotic lives and irresponsibility of some artists, who in turn pass on that pain and chaos through their music. They don't realize that their actions teach louder than their words. They sometimes say as an excuse, "I'm nobody's role model" or "I didn't ask to have the influence I do. I'm just making music." But they most certainly have the influence whether they asked for it or not. That's the major glitch in the modern music industry, the fact that talented people with little or no character training, academic training, respect or common courtesy can be catapulted to stardom and great influence with little or no accountability. That's like someone, who shows potential as a medical doctor, being given a top job at a top hospital without having to pass any tests or complete any college courses. That, my friend, is a big problem. It's a problem because you should not get to operate on people before you first sit under the tutelage of a master doctor who is highly skilled. You should not be allowed to write prescriptions for patients without first receiving years of intense formal training at an accredited college or institution of higher learning. Likewise, music artists should not be given a platform like MTV, BET or any other major network without first sitting under the tutelage and training of a master music artist who knows the business and has a track record of integrity. This is important because of the great influence that comes with being a successful recording artist.

At any rate, use your influence as a music artist in a responsible way, and you will be better for it. And never forget that your actions teach louder than words.

7. Message Carrier

Music can be a vehicle that carries various messages. Because of that, it's important to always transport thoughts and images that are true and beneficial. Let me say that again. It's important to always transport thoughts and images that are both true and beneficial. Never underestimate the power of teaching through music. How did you learn your ABC's? It's likely you did it with the help of music. Remember, music is a "quasi" universal language that can usually be understood by most people, if not everyone. Music can be used to encourage the good in us. But it can also be used to bring out the not-so-good in people, depending on the message of the song. Music can be used to help soothe our minds and create a peaceful atmosphere. But it can also be used to disrupt and create chaos. Because music is able to carry words, messages, and invoke thought, it's important that you closely monitor the music you listen to, making sure you are not inadvertently being mentally filled with the wrong thing.

8. Reading Music and Playing by Ear

Being able to read music and play by ear is important to maximizing your music potential. Certainly, you can find successful performers and songwriters, some of who cannot play by ear but they can read music; others who cannot read music but they play by ear. However, learning to do both will make you a better and more well-rounded performer and songwriter, so don't limit yourself.

Music first begins in the mind, not on paper. That means it is perfectly okay to play by ear. But to preserve the accuracy of a composer's musical thoughts, and to more easily communicate those thoughts, it is important to put music on paper. That means one should learn to read and write music also. Remember, music is a language. Babies learn to say mama and daddy by ear long before that can actually read mama and daddy on paper. This is an ancient principle, and was around long before the Suzuki Music Method came along, which purports to say the same thing. So never be ashamed of learning music by ear. It's a wonderful gift to be able to play by ear; a gift many people don't have. But keep in mind; it's ok that a six-month old baby cannot read. But it's not okay that a twenty year old cannot read! So learn to read music. It will not hurt your musical creativity. It will only enhance it.

Perfecting Your Ear

Fundamentally speaking, to play by ear means (1) being able to play the music that you hear in your mind, but without the aid of written sheet music. And (2) it means being able to assist in interpreting the musical thoughts of others. That means a person can sing a song that you've never heard before, and you (through trial and error) put music to what's being sung.

To perfect playing by ear you must first fill your mind with musical words, sentences, and paragraphs (i.e. melodies, chord progressions, and songs). In order to have music come out of you, you first must have it put into you. So learn to play the songs of others. This will broaden your musical ear and help you with your improvisation. Don't confine yourself to playing only your musical thoughts, ideas, or original songs. That will stunt your creativity and ability to play by ear. Learning the music of others will only serve to better equip you to play by ear. Think of it in these terms. If someone makes a small music deposit into your life, you can make a small music withdrawal. But if someone makes a LARGE music deposit into your life, you can make a LARGE music withdrawal. Playing by ear is simply drawing from the musical ideas and concepts that are in you. The more that's in you, the more you have to draw from.

Start With What You Know

There are no short cuts or magic tricks to playing by ear. It takes work, but you can do it! Start with something you know like Happy Birthday or another simple song of your choosing. The point is to choose a song that you're very familiar with. Why? You're trying to convert something in your mind to your instrument. If you're not familiar with the song (in your mind) how well do you think you're going to play it on your instrument? Not very well, if at all, so be sure you know the lyrics and music (in your mind) before attempting to play a song on your instrument by ear. And as you become more fluent with playing the notes you've been hearing in your mind, your ability to play by ear will automatically increase.

With consistent hard work you can eventually get to the place where you can hear a song for the first time and immediately begin playing it with a more precise trial and error approach. It's always trial and error or best guesses, but the more genres and music styles you master by ear the more fluent your trial and error process will be. So learn all the songs you can by ear and by sheet music. Start with the simple songs you know, and work your way up to the more difficult pieces.

9. Music in Other People's Heads

Learning to interpret music that is in other people's heads is an important step to perfecting your playing by ear. Don't forget. You must first learn to play what's in your mind before making an educated guess as to what's in another person's mind. Try completing the following sentences, which should give you an idea of what interpreting music in other people's minds is like. Just fill in the missing words.

The other day I was thinking about some _____ I know. I haven't seen or _____ from them in a long _____. So I decided to _____ them a _____ and send it via the United States Postal Service. Honestly, I prefer to contact them by _____. But I don't have a computer. At any rate, I sincerely _____ them and hope one _____ to be reunited and _____ _____ old times.

Here is how it should read.

The other day I was thinking about some ___one___ I know. I haven't seen or ___heard___ from them in a long ___time___. So I decided to ___write___ them a ___letter___ and send it via the United States Postal Service. Honestly, I prefer to contact them by _____email_____. But I don't have a smart phone or computer. At any rate, I sincerely _____miss_____ them and hope one ___day___ to be reunited and ___talk___ ___about___ old times.

Did you get it perfect the first time or did you make a few incorrect assumptions in your trial and error process? Most people make at least one mistake in the exercise above, like where it says: So I decided to <u>write</u> them a <u>letter</u>. When reading it the first time many people often say: So I decided to <u>give</u> them a <u>call</u>...which would have been incorrect, because the line after that makes reference to sending it via the United States Postal Service. See, that's what playing by ear is like when a musician is put on the spot in church (or anywhere else) and asked to play a song by ear (i.e. no sheet music) that he or she has never heard before. It's a best guess scenario, and you shouldn't judge a musician's greatness on whether or not he or she gets it right the first time. There are many possible combinations and any one of them could be correct, depending on what the performer is hearing in his or her head.

Ultimately, it is not prudent or kind to put a musician on the spot like that, having given no prior notice. It doesn't matter how well some musicians play by ear or read sheet music. The proper way is to rehearse ahead of time and perfect one's music before performing it publicly. Sure, there will be times when having a rehearsal prior to performance is not possible, and you'll have to make the best of it. But, whenever and wherever you can, try to do everything "decently and in order" (1 Corinthians 14:40, KJV). In other words, try to perfect your music presentations ahead of time. Even in the case where you are "flowing in the spirit" and spontaneous music and worship is taking place—something that hasn't been rehearsed—it's still important to have a track record of practicing your instrument at home so that you have perfected the skills necessary to flow in the spirit!

Secondly, understand that playing by ear for others is like filling in the gaps, similar to the example above. It's taking an educated guess as to what other people are hearing in their heads. The better you are at playing the music you hear in your mind, the better you will become at interpreting the music in other people's minds. But remember, playing by ear for others is still not an exact science, because for every single melody note another person may be hearing in their mind, there are literally hundreds of combinations of chords and notes that can be played. Having to figure out the right combination is the challenging part. Sometimes you figure it out quickly and your guess-work gets the job done. Other times your guess-work does not do the job. But don't be discouraged when that happens. Remember. The music is in their heads, not yours. You're trying to put music to what they're hearing in their minds. If the music were in *your* head, you could more easily determine whether or not the chords you are playing are correct.

Interpreting the music in other people's heads can sometimes be very tedious, especially when others are unable to musically articulate what they're hearing, and may even blame you for the music not sounding right! But that's all a part of interpreting the music in other people's heads.

10. Conclusion

I must stop right here, otherwise this book might become too lengthy to be a handbook. There are, for certain, many other chapters I wrote, which I wanted to include in this book. But these chapters, however, have been included to provide a basic overview of the three most important biblical principles of music, which I have come to understand during my nearly forty years as a musician. I am absolutely certain that these biblical principles are relevant to musicians and artists of all types, everywhere.

These principles can be summed up in this: That God made everything, including music. And there are only three things you can do with music: worship with it, entertain with it or teach it. Music worship means performing your best for God. Music entertainment means performing your best for people. And music teaching means teaching others to do both of the above, correctly and with integrity. There is a right way to do music, and a wrong way. Choose to do music the right way.

Visit carthon.org to order copies of this book for your church, school, group or private students. Discounts available for bulk orders.
Help us change a generation of musicians!

Notes